MEMORIES OF WESSEX

A BOYHOOD IN A DORSET VALLEY

RAYMOND FORCEY

DORSET BOOKS

First published in Great Britain in 1992 by Dorset Books

British Library Cataloguing in Publication Data
CIP Catalogue Record for this book
is available from the British Library.

ISBN 1 871164 16 8

DORSET BOOKS
Official Publisher to Dorset County Council
1 Chinon Court
Lower Moor Way
Tiverton EX16 6SS
Tel: 0884 243242
Fax: 0884 243325

Line illustrations are from 'Unknown Dorset' by D. Maxwell with kind permission of the publisher.

Printed and bound in Great Britain by
BPCC Wheaton Ltd, Exeter

FOREWORD

For many years I have walked the downs and valleys around Bushes Barn where the heart of this book is set. In the early 1980s I noticed a small plaque by a sapling, stating that it had been planted by R.C. Forcey who lived here 1909-1914. I wondered what tale lay behind this, and whether he was still alive. In 1987 I wrote a poem which began:

A more than half hour's walk from any road
the ruin stands, cradled in the downfold.
Ribbed pleats mitigate the strongest winds
seasonably chalk-white, green or gold.
Nearby a sapling beech commemorates
six years, 1909-1914
when R.C. Forcey lived here,
spelling in memoriam paradise. *

Subsequently I learnt from a farmer that Mr Forcey was still alive, although the farmer did not know his address. Fortunately, early in 1989, I was eventually able to obtain this, through the publican at Godmanstone. I wrote to Mr Forcey saying how much I loved that spot and enclosed my poem. He immediately responded, sending me a small typed booklet, which is the central part of this book.

Our correspondence continued and was followed by meetings, both in Dorset and once at his home in Wellingborough. I was both moved and fascinated by his account of his life at Bushes Barn (Bushes Bottom in the book) in the early years of this century, and by his additional verbal memories. Despite his long absence he still sounded

* The poem appears in full at the end of the book.

a man of Dorset. I encouraged him to add to the memoir and let it be submitted for publication. He agreed, although his modesty meant that he had, I think, little hope that it would be of interest to those whom he did not know.

Mr Forcey is now in his 89th year. After leaving Dorset at the age of 11 he lived in the Isle of Wight. He left school at 13, starting work on a farm. However, he did not wish to be bound to the land so after the war he became a driver for a bakery company and worked in the bakery industry for the remainder of his working life, becoming a bakery manager during the second war and subsequently running his own business. For many years he worked in London and the South East, but in 1961 moved to the Midlands where he has lived ever since.

He married 62 years ago. His wife died ten years ago having been an invalid for some years prior to her death. He has two sons and a daughter, eight grandchildren and six great-grandchildren. His sons have followed him into the bakery trade. Since his wife's illness and an illness of his own he has lived with his daughter who is a teacher.

He has certainly achieved his aim of not being bound to the land, being very aware of the hardships and limitations of such a life. But as this book shows, he has never lost his love for the valley where he lived as a boy. He recently told me with delight that some of the landowners in the valley intended to replant trees and allow part of the valley to regain the variety of trees, gorse and flowers which he knew and mourns. I feel privileged to have known him and value the warmth, views and memories which make this book.

Ann Elton
September 1992

Contents **Page**

A school photograph, 1913. The author is standing centre row, extreme left.

CHAPTER ONE
The Beginning

Life began for me at the tiny hamlet of Warmwell Down in the early summer of 1904. My parents were people more or less bound to the soil, father was a carter and like most farm workers of that era, was very poorly paid for long hours of work. I have no recollection of the place as we must have moved to Martinstown when I was very young. I have revisited the farm recently and had a very interesting conversation with an elderly lady who lived there. She remembered the names of many of the people whom I had heard my parents speak of. I learned from her that Mr Alfy Coleman who had always acted as a runner for the late Mr Henry Duke had been, in addition to his other activities, a land agent and no doubt it was this connection which prompted my parents to go to the Isle of Wight with Mr Coleman's son after Henry Duke died. His death at the early age of fifty-nine was a great blow to father as he had worked for the Duke family for most of his working life and I know that when we moved to Martinstown he went to work for Mr Edward Duke at Manor Farm.

This knowledge I gained later, as I have already said, I was too young to remember our move to Martinstown and my earliest memories are from the age of three.

I had a great aunt and uncle who lived in one of a row of cottages on the left hand side of the Dorchester road at Winterborne. I remember the telegraph boy bringing a telegram to the door for my mother. This brought the news of Aunt's sudden death.

I was taken up to the farm where the manager's wife looked after me while Mother went off to Winterborne and helped with all the funeral and so on. The farm manager was a Mr Stone and I remember to this day that they gave me a little brown bottle, like a Bovril bottle, full of lemonade; I must have enjoyed it immensely to remember it so clearly.

At the farm they had a big Old English sheepdog and for years my mother had a photograph of me with my arms around this dog's neck. I don't know what became of the picture. I suppose when my parents died it must of been thrown out, but I do recall the dog's name; it was Watch.

Another of my earliest memories of the village was the fair. There was a large field just beyond the school on the west and the fair took place there. I don't know if it was an annual event or whether it came more than once a year, but what I do remember are the roundabouts and coconut shies and the gingerbread stall. I was too young to take part in any of the fair's activities but I loved the gingerbread. When I visited Martinstown recently I noticed that this field has now been built over. What was the school still remains but is now the village hall, I believe.

As you enter the village, travelling west, there was a big house on the left. Here lived the Hydes. The principal thing I remember of them was that the old lady was very ill and dying so straw was spread over the road outside to deaden the noise of passing traffic, which at that time was mostly horse drawn. All through that village on the same side of the road ran a stream. It was quite deep in winter or when it rained heavily.

We lived in one of the houses on that side of the road. There is a row of cottages just past the entrance to the farm. Our house was almost opposite the school and there were little wooden bridges across the stream giving access to these houses. This brings to mind what was to me a very funny incident. It involved the grocer, a man named Johnny Fare. He had a shop in Dorchester but used to come round the village on Friday, calling for orders. These would then be delivered on Saturday. Well, one Friday evening, it had been a wet and windy day and the bridges were slippery and there was no hand rail; so Johnny Fare slipped and fell into the stream when it was in full flood; I can still hear his shouts. The language was such that in company with other children watching we were hauled off indoors.

There was another character known as old Johnny Friday who used to come through the villages with a barrel organ and a little monkey sitting on top. He stopped and played a few tunes at the bottom of school lane; whether he ever collected any money I wouldn't know but I am certain he would never have got any from the children because they had no money, ever.

Another of my earliest memories of the days before the First World War is of the town criers in Dorchester and Weymouth. In fact the town crier of Weymouth was my mother's uncle and he occupied this position for many years. I remember how on our infrequent visits to town I would see this resplendent figure come out into the street with a great bell and shout the latest news. A crowd would gather round to hear it.

One occasion I remember very clearly, I must have been four or even five at the time. A lady called at the school in a splendid car with great brass headlamps and a uniformed chauffeur. She wore a wide-brimmed hat tied down with a veil and she arranged with the teachers to give every child a ride in this car. We were all lined up outside the school and four or five of us at a time went for a ride the length of the village and back. No doubt this was the first time any of us children had a ride in a motor car. I wonder if there is anyone else alive today who shared that ride? I don't know who the lady was, but it may have been Mrs Henry Duke, as I know that Mr Duke had a car in those days.

Another of my earliest memories is of the state of the roads and the terrible dust that used to rise whenever a car came along in dry weather. Around the period from the turn of the century until the First World War cars were becoming a new means of transport. You were likely to suffer a good deal of discomfort whenever one came along a road on which you happened to be walking. There were no tarred roads at that time; they were made of gravel and flint and bound together with chalk or limestone then sprayed with water and rolled down by big steam-rollers. In dry weather they became very dusty. Slow-moving traffic such as horse carts did not stir up much dust but a car travelling at twenty miles an hour created an awful lot. The hedgerows became quite white with it and we were no longer able to pick blackberries on the roadside as they were spoilt by the dust. The surface did not stay firm for long and soon became full of potholes. After it rained these holes were full of water and if you were walking and a car or a horse and cart came along you could get drenched with muddy water.

These problems were not confined to the countryside but were even worse in the towns. There the roads would be sprayed with water every few hours in very dry weather. The water sprayers were horse drawn and would be driven by a man seated on top. They would pass up one side of the street and down the other. Shoppers on the pavement had to watch out or they would get a wetting. There were of course no street lights so if you were walking in the dark you could not see the potholes and floundered through them as likely as not.

Transport in those days was very limited although most families were self-sufficient to a degree. The only means of getting from the villages of Martinstown or Godmanstone to Dorchester was by walking or by the carrier's van which ran twice weekly. He would pick up passengers or a shopping list from residents through the villages. The number of passengers was very limited, perhaps half a dozen at the most. All the vans from the surrounding villages parked in the market place. Horses were stabled, watered and fed at the hostelry while the carrier did his shopping and he would usually begin his return journey at around five o'clock, delivering all his purchases and passengers en route. There was no bus service in those days and many villages were miles from the nearest railway station.

I remember the baker calling through the village. He had a two-wheeled cart and used to call about three times a week. The bakery was at a mill about half way from Martinstown to Winterborne and known as Gunthrip's Mill. Presumably they ground their own flour also, and the stream that runs through the village to this day must have been their source of power.

I remember too, the great four-in-hand coaches which used to run through Godmanstone. They were of course purely pleasure trips for people able to afford them, as regular coach services had long since stopped. If they happened to be passing through a village when the children came out of school the joy riders used to throw pennies out to the children. These old coaches used to seat people inside and on top, perhaps about sixteen or eighteen passengers, with the coachman dressed in frock coat and silk hat. On a platform at the rear sat the footman with a large silver trumpet which he would blow as he approached a village. In the days I am writing of this was just for show and so a novelty; years before of course this had been to announce the arrival of the coach at the post house.

I do remember well the few occasions on which we walked from Martinstown to Dorchester; these excursions only took place in summer. My two elder sisters and my brother, with my baby sister in the old wickerwork pram, would set out early in the morning. Our first call on arrival was at our grandmother's house in Dukes Avenue. Here we would have a rest and then accompany mother to do the shopping. The girls usually stayed with Grandma while my brother and I went on the understanding that if we behaved ourselves the reward would be a slice of a type of Christmas pudding at the Soldier's Home just at the top of Friary Hill, by the gaol. This cost one penny a slice and how we enjoyed it.

When you went shopping in those days, everything you required such as rice, lentils, sugar or dried peas were weighed and packed in thick, blue paper bags while you waited. There were no pre-packed goods. If you bought biscuits they were loose in a large tin and weighed up for you. We never went to greengrocers as we grew everything we needed in our own garden. Shoe shops and outfitters' shops had a system of handling money which always fascinated me; when the customer handed the cash to the assistant it was then placed in a cup on a wire which ran across the shop to the office. The assistant would pull a cord and the cup would fly across to the office; shortly afterwards it would return with the change. It was also the custom at that time in outfitters to give a packet of pins rather than a farthing change. So if you bought an article costing eleven pence three farthings and tendered a shilling you were never given a farthing but pins instead.

I have learnt in the years since that Dorchester did have a few industries apart from farming and engineering. One was button making which I knew nothing of at the time I lived there. Another was rope and net making; the latter I remember well as my dear old grandmother toiled for years making nets for the fishermen at Portisham and West Bay. It was the only means she had of a livelihood as my grandfather had perished in a blizzard in 1881 when my mother was eleven. She was the eldest of a family of five children so one does not need to have a very vivid imagination to appreciate that Grandma had an enormous task to survive and bring up her family. But she did it. As a boy when we went to visit her I used to fill her wooden needles with the twine she used for netting. This twine was supplied by the company she worked for. She did not get a wage but was paid a commission for work done. My sister still has some of the wooden needles she used.

At the bottom of Friary Hill on the left was a little house where my Uncle Harry and Aunt Mary lived. It was a funny little house with an archway running under one bedroom to allow the continuation of a footpath which passed under the archway and turned right through a little wicket gate into the tiny garden beside which the river ran. On the other side of the footpath was a strip of land where my uncle kept his chickens. I remember how he always went into the chicken run on his return from work and turned the bottoms of his trousers down; they were always full of corn. As I grew older I understood the reason for this. He worked at Eldridge and Pope's brewery where he had to shovel barley for the beer with a large wooden shovel. During the course of this his deep turn-ups filled with grain with which he fed his chickens.

After shopping had been completed and farewells taken of Grandma we would start the long walk home. My mother had a system for getting us home without too much grizzling because we were tired. She would have a ball and roll it along ahead of us, encouraging us to race after it, and then when we reached it to sit and wait for her to overtake us. Thus our trips to town were completed. Looking back though, I have often wondered how as children we managed to walk these distances, I can't imagine children doing it today. It is three miles from Martinstown to Dorchester.

Later still when we lived at Bushes Bottom we could go by train but we still had a mile and a half to walk to the station. I think the memory which remains clearest of this journey was the return in winter when it was dark. We would board the train just as it was getting dark, take our seats and then hear footsteps overhead. A porthole would open in the roof of the carriage and a paraffin lamp would be lowered to hang. This was the means of lighting in those days.

Grimstone station has gone now, but I noticed the track lines are still there.

CHAPTER TWO

Bushes Bottom

I shall try to paint a picture of Bushes Bottom as seen through the eyes of a lad who lived there between the ages of five and ten-and-a-half.

We came to this valley in the summer of 1909 from Martinstown where I had started school at the age of three. We had enjoyed certain services in this village, such as a main road, a carrier's van which ran to Dorchester twice weekly, mains water, and the school only a few yards across the road from where we lived. But here at Bushes Bottom there was no road, only a cart track and bridle path from Grimstone in one direction and to Godmanstone in the other. The track to Godmanstone was the more difficult as there was a very steep chalk hill to climb and it was about one-and-a-half miles to the village.

The distance to Grimstone was slightly more than this. We walked from Martinstown and approached the valley from Grimstone. On turning off the Sydling road we entered a short lane which led to a small farmstead run by a Mr Gifford and his three sons. A cart track and bridle path led from here northward up the valley. On our left we came to a wood, quite a substantial size; the trees were mostly fir and pine. This extended about four hundred yards and at the end there was a gateway through a tall thick hedge which extended right up the valley. We had to go through this gate to follow the path which led to the farmstead of Bushes Bottom. On our left was rising ground as far as one could see. The part nearest the path was covered with gorse. Beyond this was grass stretching away to the horizon and on this area cattle were grazing. I learned later that about one hundred Red Devon steers, one or two shire colts and sheep were left to roam these hills and feed on the grass. This in itself made a lovely picture but it was the valley which was so beautiful, the trees, the bushes, the gorse and wild flowers beggar description. And the wildlife, well, I had never seen so many rabbits, and even in broad daylight we saw several foxes, stoats and weasels. I don't think that one could every forget those first impressions of that lovely valley. It was wild and primitive but to a child of my age it was awe-inspiring.

We eventually reached the farmstead; our house was the first of a pair of cottages adjacent to the farmyard. This, by today's standards, was also very primitive. On the ground floor there was just one large room and a small pantry. The floor itself was of large hexagonal shaped stones; there was a very large open fireplace and built into the wall to the left of this was an oven which was heated when required, by wood and faggots.

Stairs led from the ground floor to a tiny landing and three bedrooms, the largest of these had a fireplace. Our family numbered seven.

This farmstead was nestled in a break in the main valley which extended about half a mile west, while the main valley continued northward towards Sydling. At this time all the land was farmed by a very well-known farmer and landowner of the time, Mr Henry Duke. He had, I later understood, formed an auctioneer's business a few years before the turn of the century, as also did a certain Gyles Symonds and others, to enable them to market their products more satisfactorily. At this time, I believe, Henry Duke controlled some seventeen thousand acres. Be that as it may, he was a considerate employer.

My father was a carter and he looked after four very fine shire horses. Three he drove himself, the fourth was used for odd jobs about the farm carting hay or straw or any other requirements for the cattle.

The valley at this time was open country as far as the eye could see, dotted with trees, gorse and bushes, while the grass was grazed short by the cattle. In addition to the cattle already mentioned there was one black and white cow which provided milk for the families who lived in the farmstead. This gave us all a plentiful supply of milk and butter. We did have one facility we had not expected. This was mains water. This was not so surprising really because there was no water in the valley and all these cattle had to have water. The residents shared one tap which was against the stable wall and the cattle were catered for by several large tanks controlled by ballcocks. There was also a large well near the stables and the men from the families always got water from this for washing day and, no doubt, in earlier times it had been the only water available. But it would have been quite impossible to supply the needs of all this livestock from this well only in the days of which I write. One of the big water tanks was situated down by the wagon shed and is still there. I doubt if it is the same tank but there is one in the same place.

The cattle that roamed the hills and pasture land were rounded up in the autumn. This was done by Mr Smith, the farm manager, who lived at Godmanstone. He would come with two of this stockmen, all mounted on horses; the cattle would be driven down from the surrounding hills into the yard, and would be selected; those ready for market would be penned in the cowshed and the others would be freed. Those retained would be fed on cake, hay etc. until they had put on more weight. After about a month they would be driven off to market, presumably for the Christmas beef trade.

It is difficult to convey in words the beauty of the valley as it was then; the variety of trees, bushes and wild flowers had to be seen to be believed. In spring the hedgerows were a blaze of colour with primroses, wild violets, horse daisies, cowslips and daffodils. I could never understand how great clumps of daffodils came to be growing wild. They must have been planted at some time. The hedges themselves were red and white may, dog roses and honeysuckle. When they were in bloom it was a magnificent sight. Later in the season foxgloves grew in abundance.

Winter in the valley was pretty grim as I remember: that long walk to school in the bitter cold and the rain and sometimes the snow. There were days in winter when we just couldn't get to school, but even then a certain wild beauty remained. One of my most vivid memories is of going to school in the early winter mornings when there had been a hard frost and the gorse bushes and trees were festooned with cobwebs which glistened with the frost and looked like fairyland. Another was the bird chorus in the spring. A wide variety of birds lived in the valley including jays, thrushes, blackbirds, bullfinches; and I have never seen a place where so many goldfinches lived, on spring mornings they sang so much you could hardly hear yourself speak.

There were also a lot of owls. They mostly lived in the barn but after dark they would fly around the trees and bushes and a constant hooting went on. This, with the distant yapping of foxes, was a nightly chorus which we became accustomed to.

Also on summer evenings, just as it was getting dark, the bats that lived in the barn would come out and fly round. We used to throw our caps at them in the hope of bringing one down but never with any success.

Foxes were numerous. My father kept chickens and I remember him having a constant battle trying to protect them. The pen and chicken house had to be very strong and foolproof. My younger sister had a pet rabbit and in spite of all our efforts to protect it the foxes had it one night.

Great care had to be taken in those days in the valley as it abounded with snakes; slow-worms and grass snakes were not dangerous but adders were very prolific and in the winter they would often conceal themselves in the barn or stable loft.

Another thing I remember was a family of wild cats, very large ginger cats and extremely wild and vicious. I imagine they must have been descended from tame cats of an earlier resident and being left to fend for themselves had become wild.

I feel that this only emphasises the wildness and beauty of the valley as it was then, totally unspoilt by man. But would anyone live there today under the conditions in which we lived? I doubt it. But looking back I think that the happy memories remain where the more unpleasant ones tend to stay in the background of one's mind - such as struggling home from school wet through, or through inches of snow. Such seem best forgotten as there was no enjoyment in them.

Bushes Bottom from a sketch by the author.

CHAPTER THREE

The Farmstead

This was built to form a large square; the two cottages, the five-barred gate and the stables formed the front, at the rear of the cottages on the left was a long open cowshed with a tiled roof. The houses were slate roofed. Across the rear was the barn and built on to the barn on the left was a building with a sloping roof and double doors at the rear. This may have been a shelter for a pony trap or cart for earlier residents, probably when the farmhouse was occupied by the farmer and his family. On the right hand side of the barn was a brick wall which linked up with the farmhouse, this being much bigger than the other two cottages, and joining the rear right hand corner of the stables, thus making an enclosed yard or compound. This was always known to us children as the Barken. Whether this is a word still used in Dorset I cannot say but it remains as such to me.

The barn was always stacked to the roof, on one side with straw and on the other with hay, cattle cake, a chaff cutter and a mangle cutter. In winter, when the weather was very bad, the gate to this yard was left open so that the cattle could take shelter and be fed.

I have already described our house interior; the adjoining one was the same but the farmhouse was much bigger. Here there were two large rooms and a large pantry on the ground floor, the floor itself being the same big hexagonal stones as in the other cottages; upstairs there were four bedrooms.

Each house had a large garden with blackcurrent and gooseberry bushes, rhubarb and so on. At the bottom was a large wagon shed which ran the length of the gardens. This housed all the wagons, carts and farm implements. In those days these were taken great care of and on wet days, when the men were unable to work on the land, they would spend their time cleaning and greasing these ready for further use.

The stables housed four horses; they were shires, very large fine animals with great white fetlocks. They were my father's responsibility. He always took a great pride in his horses. I remember mother jokingly saying on more than one occasion that he thought more of his horses than of her. He would never sit down to a meal until they had been cared for. They were well fed and always looked fine. I have always thought of them since as gentle giants.

When the stables were cleaned out daily all this went into the Barken and together with the straw and cattle droppings produced a considerable amount of dung. This was usually cleared after the harvest was over and spread on the land. This meant several days' hard work for all hands. It all had to be loaded with forks by hand and spread in the same way as there were no mechanical loaders or spreaders in those days. Another point was that there were no arable fields within half a mile of the farm. This meant a long haul for the horses and carts. As soon as this was completed fresh straw would be strewn in the yard in preparation for the cattle selected as I have already described.

The only form of lighting we had in those days was paraffin and candles. The stables were lit by a hurricane lamp hung from a beam and the houses by paraffin lamps with glass globes, and always candles for bedtime.

There was only one door to the cottages, that was the front door, so everything had to be brought in that way, firewood, faggots for the oven, everything. This couldn't have helped to make life easier for my mother in her efforts to keep the house clean and tidy.

At the rear of the house the roof sloped down over an outhouse with an earth floor; here we stored wood and potatoes, etc. In the pantry was a bench covered in slate and on this my mother kept a large shallow pan into which she poured our share of the milk. When this had settled she would skim off the cream for butter making, a process which I will explain later.

This then is how I remember the farmstead of Bushes Bottom.

CHAPTER FOUR

The Dwellers in the Valley

At that time, which was prior to the First World War, three families lived here. In the farmhouse lived a family of ten, Mr and Mrs Budden, their five sons, Joe, Harry, Charlie, Fred and George, the latter being the same age as myself. Then their three daughters who were all still at school, Elizabeth, Alice and Florence. The eldest son, Joe, was in the army so we didn't see much of him. Next was Harry who was a very backward fellow, something of a simpleton. The others were all perfectly normal.

I remember Mrs Budden was a very big woman and I always remember Mr Budden for his sideboards. I think, looking back, that they must have had a very hard life. They never seemed to live as well as we did and often the only kind of sandwiches they brought to school for their dinner was bread and lard.

Next door to us lived Mr and Mrs Sandford who were very nice. They were a young couple with no children. My mother and Mrs Sandford shared in the care of the pretty flower border which ran the length of the two houses.

As I have already said there were seven in my family so the total living there at the time was nineteen and there always seemed to be a spirit of friendliness existing between the families. So much had to be shared such as the milk, pig killing, shopping, gathering fuel and so on that I suppose that it was essential for survival.

CHAPTER FIVE

How we Lived in Those Days

I suppose my family would have been described as average. There were five of us children from the time of my earliest memories. My eldest sister Lillian was ten years older than me; Louise came next being two years younger than her and then Victor who was two years younger again. My youngest sister was three years younger than me.

The majority of the cottages in which families like ours lived were of the same design. On the ground floor was one room with a small pantry and a large open fireplace. Most of the cottages had an oven built into the wall at the side of the fireplace where the bread could be baked. In some I have visited in recent years I notice that the fireplace has been reduced in size and a brick built hob has been installed including a small oven.

The first floor was usually divided into three bedrooms. One of these almost always had an open fireplace, mainly I suppose because the chimney breast from downstairs ran up through the bedroom. This could be lit in the event of sickness. I remember that at that time a popular way of dealing with bronchitis was a steam kettle. This had a very long spout; the fire would be lit and the kettle brought to the boil and the steam emitted was supposed to help the patient's breathing. I have no idea whether this was a satisfactory means of treatment or not.

The normal furnishings of a house in those days was as follows. The stone floor was partly covered with a square of coconut matting. In the centre of the room was a large wooden table, six or seven chairs, a sofa usually home-made, and what was known as a chiffonier. This was a two door cupboard with a very high back on which were three shelves. On the edge of these shelves was a row of hooks from which the cups and jugs were hung; the plates and saucers stood on the shelves and the food was stored in the cupboards beneath. Over the fireplace was a mantel-piece and on this stood the clock which had to be wound up nightly. That was always my father's last job before retiring to bed.

In the bedrooms the furniture consisted of a double bed and perhaps a single depending on the number in the family. There were no wardrobes or cupboards. Any spare clothes you possessed were stored in a wooden box with a lid. Bed linen and clean washing was kept in an article called an ottoman which usually stood on the tiny landing.

Most of the houses like ours were very draughty. I remember my father made a screen to stand inside the door and mother covered it with hessian which she dyed for this purpose.

* * *

I look back over the past to those days and realise how very lucky I and my brother and sisters were. We had good parents. Mother was a wonderful cook and manager. Father never drank or smoked. I never knew him to visit a public house in his life, but to say he never smoke or drank is not quite true for I remember him telling me once that he had smoked a clay pipe but when the price of tobacco increased to two pence an ounce he decided to give it up. As for drinking I remember that my mother used to brew homemade beer in the summer and as children we used to take a large earthenware jug to the harvest fields on a hot day. This was shared by all the men working there. but that is as far as my father ever drank. Consequently all his earnings were devoted to the family budget.

Now this was an area where there was much distress. The money just would not go round and I can remember as a lad often hearing my father and mother argue as to how they were going to pay for this or that. It must have been a problem. Nonetheless in all our growing up I can honestly say that we were never left hungry. Maybe we were not as well clothed as we would have wished, mainly because clothes had to be handed down. We younger ones never had anything new. That is why I so clearly remember the incident which I will describe later of my finding a tiny purse containing five gold sovereigns on the rabbit warren, and of my mother's emotion when the farm bailiff told my father to keep it. We were all fitted out in new boots and clothing for this five pounds represented five weeks' wages. It is an event I can never forget. It is impossible to convey the relief that was expressed by my parents.

As for the clothes we wore they were very different from those worn today. Boys and men wore thick woollen stockings which came over the knee, and knickerbocker trousers. Over the stockings we wore leather gaiters which buttoned. We wore these all winter and much of the summer because of the danger of adder bites. There were many snakes in the valley and no antidote to the poison in those days. Women wore woollen stockings and long boots which also buttoned. So every household had to have a buttonhook. Boys and men wore heavy hobnail boots, there were no wellington boots in those days. Every evening my father would inspect our boots to see if any of the hobs were missing; if they were he would get his last out and replace them. In those days you could buy these hobnails on a card and also what were known as Blakey's Protectors which were another type of nail used extensively on boots worn in country districts. The boots themselves cost three shillings and sixpence a pair. To get a pair soled and heeled cost one shilling and sixpence. I know that well because my Uncle Sid who lost a leg in the First World War was taught shoemaking as a rehabilitation occupation. He lived at Winterbourne Abbas and when I visited him a few years later I learnt that it had been a complete waste of training because he could not possibly earn a living repairing boots and shoes in a remote village with a population of about two hundred people. So he had to eke out his very poor disability pension getting any small employment he could.

We had Norfolk type jackets. In school I remember that the girls wore frilly pinafores in class. Everyone wore a hat. The most popular head dress for men was a bowler or a cap; women usually favoured very wide-brimmed hats and kept them on by using hatpins pushed through their hair. In those days women wore corsets and these had steel springs in them. When they were discarded we boys used to collect the springs from them as they made jolly good pea shooters. If you could take a few of these to school you were very popular with the other lads if not with the teachers.

You can imagine how cold it often was in winter; not only outside but also in the house. Getting up was a very chilly business, having to dress in a bitterly cold bedroom and go down to a room where the fire had just been lit and the warmth had hardly penetrated. Mother used to wash and scrub us in this atmosphere. There were often tears. But there never was such a thing as a toothbrush in the house and no dental care. Mother used to suffer terribly from toothache but we could never afford a dentist. After we moved to the Isle of Wight she had all her teeth out. I and all my sisters and brother had lost all our own teeth by the age of twenty six or so.

Our nearest doctor was at Cerne Abbas and provision had been made for those living at Bushes; there was a little white cob who roamed with the other horses who could be caught and ridden to get help in an emergency. He was not very co-operative and was very difficult to catch so a small weight on a chain was strapped to one foreleg which prevented him galloping off and so made it easy to catch him.

I had the misfortune one day when I was in the loft of the stables to fall through the trap door into the stables below and landed head first among some plough shares that lay there. I suffered a slight fracture of the skull and my father had to catch the pony and ride to Cerne Abbas for the doctor. He came, as always, on horseback. He was a good doctor and under his care I soon recovered. Some years back an acquaintance of mine wrote a book on Cerne Abbas and the surrounding villages and at the end he devoted a chapter to Dr Dalton. All I know is that he was a good doctor who never charged the poor for his services and when he died it was found that in his will he had donated his body to Bristol University for medical research.

When we arrived home from school Mother always had a bowl of hot water and we were required to wash our hands thoroughly before sitting down to our evening meal. If it was summer we would then go out to play until darkness fell and we then lined up to have a good wash. This wasn't left to us. My mother would wash our faces and hands thoroughly before we went off to bed. In the morning it was the same ritual, she never left us to wash ourselves. Friday night was bath night. A galvanised tin bath was placed in front of the fire and the big black boiler suspended over the fire full of boiling water. Father always had a couple of pails of cold water ready and would go and refill them as necessary. We each took our turn in the bath and the water was changed for each child. After this we had a dose of liquorice powder (how I hated that!) and went off to bed. In those days there were no pyjamas, we wore nightshirts.

After we had gone to bed my parents followed the same routine. My father always shaved at night. I remember that he never had a shaving mug; he used to use half a coconut shell and of course an old cut-throat razor. There were no safety razors in those days. He always used to sharpen his razor on his hand; it sounds absurd today but that was how he did it.

The idea of diet in those days had not been heard of. Our principal food was bread and home-made jam or butter, never the two together. A cow was kept to supply milk for the three families. This of course had to be cared for and milked by the menfolk and the milk was then shared. We always had butter from the milk and mother used to make jam. There were plenty of wild strawberries in the valley and of course there were more blackberries than we could use. I don't think there are nearly so many today. For breakfast in winter we had porridge; occasionally a boiled egg on Sunday mornings when the hens were laying well.

Each family had a row of potatoes in the potato field and also one of field-turnips. I suppose looking back and remembering how carefully my parents preserved our potato crop these must have been our staple diet. I certainly remember how my father used to carry on if the peel was taken off too thickly and how he tried to avoid potatoes with what he called deep eyes as they meant a lot of waste. We grew all kinds of vegetables in the garden, beans, onions, cabbage, cauliflower and peas. We did not ever have leeks. One of Mother's favourite dishes was turnips with butter. Mushrooms grew in profusion on Magiston Hill and made a fine addition to our diet.

Each family kept a pig. The pigs ran loose in the farmyard and ate vegetable peelings. But we kept them in turn so that about every three months the pig was killed and the meat shared between the three families on the farm. The pig was killed professionally; Mr Stone was the slaughterer and came to do the job properly. Of course you couldn't kill a pig between about May and September, or only in a month with an R in it, because the meat would not keep. Even later on it was difficult to keep for long so for about a week we would have roast dinner most days. My mother salted the belly. Then she would add a piece of the salted belly to rabbit stew. With the offal she made sausages, faggots, blackpudding and chitterlings.

There was often rabbit to eat because there were so many in the valley. We were allowed to catch as many as we liked and this provided a valuable source of meat. After we moved to the Isle of Wight the vicar's wife came to call on my mother and said something about rabbit. My mother said;

Rabbit hot and rabbit cold,
rabbit young and rabbit old,
rabbit bald and rabbit stuffed,
thank the Lord I've had enough.

The vicar's wife looked at her in some astonishment.

As well as keeping a pig we had hens. They were penned strongly because of the foxes. My mother would boil up potato peelings and feed them on those with skimmed milk and a little cattle cake. We always had eggs and at Christmas a fine cockerel.

My mother baked our own bread as did the women of the other families. She did this on Wednesdays and baked enough for a week. This was the pattern of the operation:

when we children came out of school on Tuesday afternoon we would collect a can of brewer's yeast from the Smith's Arms. This had to be carried out rather carefully and not tossed about too much or it would froth up and bubble over and much of it would be lost. When we arrived home with this it was placed in the cool pantry until just before bedtime, when my mother would pour it into a very large earthenware pan and the total amount of water required for the mix was added. The next thing was to add half the required amount of flour. This was thoroughly mixed, covered with a clean cloth and left for eight hours. The next morning, after the children had been got off to school, the other half of the flour and the salt was added, and again this had to be mixed very thoroughly and left for another hour. During this time the oven would be filled with wood and gorse faggots and lit and fired until it became white hot. It was then 'scuffled' out with a wet sack on the end of a pole to clear the bottom of ashes. In the meantime the dough had been divided and moulded into shape and left to rise. When it had doubled its size it was placed in the oven on a wooden peel, this was a home-made tool something like a shovel, and each loaf was placed in its desired position in this way and left to bake for forty-five minutes. This produced beautiful bread which kept well too. This process which I have described was known as the sponge method of bread making.

All other cooking had to be done over the large open fire and was managed in the following manner. Built into the chimney was a large iron hook and on this hook we hung a big black cast-iron boiler. All vegetables were cooked in nets in the same pot; these nets were specially designed for this job and could be bought. Some had very fine mesh for peas and such like, others larger for cabbage, etc. The tops were tied with a string attached and when they were dropped into the boiler these strings were left hanging over the side and made fast by placing the lid on tightly. This made it easier to get them out when the vegetables were cooked.

Now to explain what happened to our share of the milk. My mother always poured it into a very large shallow pan standing on the slate slab in the pantry. After a few hours she would take a large spoon and skim off the cream, transfer the milk to a jug and wash the pan ready for the next milking. This was repeated twice daily and the cream poured into a big glass sweet-jar. When this jar was half full the stopper was covered with a cloth to make a tight fit and it was then shaken till it turned to butter. This task was usually reserved until all the family were at home as it was a pretty tough job to keep shaking this bottle. But it was quite successful and as a consequence we always had plenty of fresh butter.

It must be remembered that no tradesmen of any sort ever came to Bushes Bottom. Those who lived there were completely isolated, therefore a bond grew up between the families to help one another, especially in the matter of shopping. Over the hill in Godmanstone there was a little general shop and if anyone required anything on Saturday that had been forgotten on schooldays, they would always call to ask if anything was needed in the other houses. But the greatest co-operation came when a trip to Dorchester became necessary to replenish supplies of flour and other essentials. This was mainly overcome by an agreement that all would return to Grimstone station by the same train and my father would take the horse and cart to meet them and thus get them home.

All letters had to be collected from Godmanstone Post Office as did the weekly newspaper, the *Western Gazette.* This was the only paper we used to have. There was of course no radio and no phone and news of any importance always reached us days late. But what did it matter? Life was slow and easy in those days.

It is almost impossible to comprehend that up to the outbreak of the First World War, I and others who attended school in Godmanstone or lived in remote country districts of Dorset knew little of the outside world. We had an occasional trip to Dorchester and once a year were taken to Weymouth on a school outing. Up to the age of ten-and-a-half I had never even seen a cricket bat or a football let alone had a chance to learn to play the games. There were no sports at those country schools in those days and in fact no playground except the lane leading up to the church.

We had very few toys. One Christmas I remember getting a kite and my brother and I had a little wind-up train set. My sisters had dolls. There were never presents or cards at birthdays. My mother had a few books. She was very fond of Dickens and I recall her reading *Nicholas Nickleby* and the *Pickwick Papers.* She would also read to us a book called *Mrs Brown and her Luggage.*

I know that I had a mouth organ; I don't remember

how I came by it, probably it was given to me by an aunt who lived in Dorchester. But I learnt to play it and still can. Sometimes I would go to visit the Giffords, a kindly old couple who lived in a smallholding at the south end of the valley, and I always got a penny for playing them a tune. Their sons had emigrated to Canada as there was no living for them in Dorset. As I have mentioned elsewhere my older cousin Ralph had a gramophone.

In wet weather we had a few games such as Snakes and Ladders and Ludo which we played. There were never playing cards in the house. Father had an old organ with bellows and roller with hymn tunes on them and he would sometimes play that. We were too far from Godmanstone to go to church on Sundays regularly so Father would play and we had our own little service. Once we moved to the Isle of Wight my parents were regular church attenders and we children went to Sunday school. But in Dorset days we only went when taken from school.

Of course we had plenty of entertainment out of doors. We children used to go adder hunting. We would put the dead snakes on a string to bring them home but were always told never to touch them until the sun went down as they were believed not to die until then. In spring we went birds' nesting but were only allowed to take one egg from each nest and not to tell anyone else where a nest was. And we never took eggs from a robin's nest because if you did that your fingers would grow crooked.

We children would look forward to certain events on the farm. Sheep shearing was one such time. We loved to watch the men capture a sheep, turn it on its back and start to clip off the wool. Of course in those days it was all done with hand clippers so it was a hard job and a slow one. If you go to the valley at Bushes Barn and look you will still see the handle of a pair of shears buried in the trunk of one of the three large ash trees there. I should imagine that some fifty years or so ago a shearer placed his shears there after he finished shearing and forgot them. The trunk has grown round them so that only the tip of the handles now show. This confirms the remoteness of the valley; no one found them before they were buried in the tree.

I now realise having reached my eighty-sixth year the effects that this isolated way of life had on us children. Despite our happiness we were handicapped by poor education, poverty and most of all by a complete lack of knowledge of what life was like in the towns. It was only when I moved from Dorset to the Isle of Wight that I began to realise the difference. My older brother and sisters suffered more and my brother, who was four years older, never managed to adapt. My younger sisters adapted best to the change. It is difficult to explain but when you found yourself in the company of others you felt inadequate and unable to mix. In another way it was like coming out of a dark tunnel into the daylight; certainly the teachers I had in the Isle of Wight were much better than in Godmanstone; and as the school was only a quarter of a mile away along a proper road we could attend regularly.

However I do not think that I understood till I was past twenty-one that this was an entirely different world from the one I had been brought up in. The trust which was paramount on the land did not prevail in industry or the business world. On the land bargains had been sealed on a handshake and were kept.

In the summer of 1916 I and several other boys of my age were asked to leave school and go to work on the land, replacing men who had been called up for military service. Conscription had been introduced and the loss of men in the battle of the Somme was causing some concern. So there I was back on the land for the princely sum of six shillings a week, working ten hours daily for six days a week. This continued until the spring of 1918 when I got the opportunity to leave the land and work for a contractor driving a horse and trolley and collecting washing, which I took from a private laundry to the naval hospital at Yarmouth in the Isle of Wight. By this time my parents had moved to Totland and we had a very nice house and garden. My father was still employed as a carter at a local farm, as was my brother.

Six months after the end of the war I left the land; I say this because I still considered while working for this contractor that it was half agriculture and I wanted to be totally free of the land and its way of life. So I applied for a job at a local bakery to drive a van and deliver bread daily on a round. I got this job and my duties were as follows: I commenced work at six a.m. in the bakery, had breakfast at seven-thirty, at eight loaded the van with the trays of bread and cakes and then delivered them to two branch shops. Then I had to take a load of bread and cakes to Golden Hill Fort to the N.A.C.B. When this was done I began my round, finishing at about five or later depending on how busy I was. For this I received fifteen shillings a week.

Now I must try to explain how my upbringing in the country was affecting me. My dialect was the object of much amusement among those with whom I worked and, as I have said earlier, I felt totally inadequate in their company. But I realised that this was a handicap I had to overcome and eventually I did so but it took a long time. I suppose that the greatest help I received in this respect was the opportunity offered me by my employer at the end of that first summer. He called me into his office one afternoon and pointed out that the end of the season had come and, to use his words, 'we were facing a black winter'. He suggested that as I knew the country districts well and was also well known there I might try to build a round selling bread and cakes. I agreed and began the following week; three days were to be the days for the country round. I was still to do the deliveries to the shops, but was to get two pence in the shilling for all the takings on the country round. Well, I was very successful. In a few short weeks I had built up quite a substantial round and was earning nearly 1 in commission. I was then told by my employer that in future my commission would only be paid on cakes sold and not on bread and flour as he didn't consider it fair to the other roundsmen. There was nothing I could do about it, I just had to accept it but I never forgot it.

Nor have I ever forgotten the treatment I received after seven years service. I had been told that no credit was to be given to a certain family who happened to be my last call on the country round. One evening I arrived at the customer who had four little children; they were all crying and when I enquired what was wrong I learnt that they were hungry. The mother told me that her husband had been to market that day with two pigs which were ready for sale; the market was dead and the pigs hadn't sold, therefore they had no money and no food as they had depended entirely on the sale of these pigs to provide the money to live on. She pleaded with me to let her have some bread so I gave way on the promise that she would pay me when they sold the pigs the following week. Well the next time they didn't sell, so I helped them out again; in the meantime I had to do something to account for the goods she had had, so I booked them out to a very reliable customer whose credit would never be questioned. The debt now owed by this family amounted to 3 and the following week I was due to go on my week's holiday. This was in October 1925. I explained to the chap who always did holiday relief what I had done and asked him to leave it till I returned.

Unfortunately I was unaware that he envied me my job as by this time I had built up the round to the stage which merited a motor van, which I had for about six months. Therefore he told my employer that the person to whom I had booked the goods denied owing it, which was of course true, but he failed to tell the whole story and so made it look as if I had taken the money for my own use. As a consequence when I returned to work on the Monday I was given a week's notice. I cycled out to see the customer and get her help as I thought that if she came forward and explained that she owed the money I would probably get a ticking off but would clear my name.

Unfortunately when I told her that I had been sacked because of helping her she immediately said 'Well, if that's how he treated you he can whistle for his money.' I explained to her that if she adopted this attitude it would not help me but she was adamant; perhaps being so desperately poor she saw it as a way of escaping her obligations, but it let me down completely. I could not now go to my employer and tell him the truth for fear that if approached the woman would completely deny it and I should look to be in a worse position than ever. So I just had to accept it and after seven years' hard and faithful service that was the outcome.

Times were very hard. I called then on my customers who were living on parish relief, this meant that when I called they would hand me a coupon for so many pounds of bread. These coupons were issued by the Parish Relieving Officer and could be cashed by the receiver at his office. This was in the early 1920s. This experience decided me that the only person to work for in future for seventy or eighty hours a week was myself, but it was many years before this was possible.

This story illustrates the results of the lack of experience of people's behaviour in the world outside. Although I had reached the age of twenty-one I still suffered perhaps unconsciously, the inability to understand that I was living in an entirely different world. I began to realise that the trust which had been paramount on the land did not prevail in industry or business; it appeared to me that it was every man for himself and the devil take the hindmost. But in spite of this realisation I could not go through life never trusting anyone. One cannot alter nature and as a consequence I have suffered many disappointments and losses throughout life, but that is another story.

CHAPTER SIX

Life on the Farms

I have already mentioned that most of the men in the village worked on the farms. I think a situation had developed over many years that once you worked on a farm you were more or less committed to this way of life for all time. I had of course first hand knowledge of my father's duties. He would start work at six in the morning and go to the stables where it was his job to look after four horses. They had to be groomed, fed and watered prior to being harnessed for the day's work which normally began at about seven-thirty. At that time the men usually stopped for what was known in Dorset lingo as 'Namit'. This consisted of cold tea (no thermos in those days), bread and, if they were lucky, a little butter or an onion. This was a ten-minute break and had to be strictly adhered to. Work on the land then continued until 2 p.m. for the carters. It may have been ploughing or dung carting, of which there was much more in those days then now. Then there was other work such as harrowing or rolling, all part of the cultivation of the land. In summer there would be grass cutting and carting the hay, then harvesting. During the summer months the horses were turned out to graze in the afternoon when they had finished work. When this happened it meant that my father had to get up earlier in the morning in order to go out and catch them. In the main this was not difficult, but there would always be one or two who were tricky to catch.

I remember one in particular who always led him a dance. This horse was named Captain. He was a beautiful great shire horse and he would wait until father got quite close to him, then would turn and kick his heels in the air and run off about fifty yards or so, turn round and wait till father approached him again then repeat the performance. In the end the only way father found that he could deal with him was to hobble him. Whilst this did not prevent him moving about freely it certainly stopped him running off.

The carters stopped work on the land at two o'clock while the other workers continued till five. The carters then came back to the stables, fed the horses and had their own dinner. They then returned to the stables to groom and care for the horses, cut chaff and clean the stables and the harness. This usually took up till five o'clock. But the day did not end there for the men who cared for the horses. At seven they would return to the stable to do what was known in Dorset terms as 'rack up'. This meant bedding the horses' stall down with straw and ensuring that all was well for the night. The only day on which they did not go out to work was Sunday but the horses still had to be groomed and cared for on that day.

The same hours applied to the cowman and his assistant. They had to milk the cows in the morning and again in the afternoon. When milking was finished in the afternoon the cows would be driven back to the pasture in summer, and in winter they had to be fed and bedded down.

All the cows had names and the name of each was printed in large letters above a stall in the cowshed. Believe it or not, when the cows were driven in they always went to the correct stall. Any old farmer will confirm it. The horses were the same. They always went to their own stall. If the cowman had a big herd of say forty cows he had a pretty hard job, especially in winter when they were kept in. As well as the feeding, cleaning and milking he and his assistant had to separate the milk and help churn the butter twice weekly. The milk had to be put through a cooler and then through a separator because on outlying farms they did not send the milk away, as they do now. They kept a certain amount to supply the local population. The cowman had to go round the village with a large can and a pint pot and half pint pot calling from door to door. He would then measure out the amount people required into their own jugs. The remainder of the milk having been separated was fed to the pigs and the cream stored for several days in a cool room then churned into butter. This task was usually done by the farmer's wife but if she was not available the task fell to the cowman again.

When the butter was made the farmer's wife and an assistant would weigh it off in one pound pieces and pat it into shape with wooden spatulas. It would then be packed in a metal tray and taken to the nearest town to be sold to the grocer.

As the cowman also had to look after any pigs kept by the farmer he had a pretty full day. And in those days there was no such thing as overtime or set working hours.

Looking back to those far off days I think that mention should be made of the life of a shepherd. He might well be in charge of a flock of perhaps two or three hundred sheep. Those were the days of what we now call organic farming; but at that time it was the only way of farming. Sheep played a very important part in this process. Crops were rotated in order to feed the sheep, white turnips, swedes or clover. The sheep were penned in with wattle hurdles, the number of sheep regulating the size of the pen. They would feed on the crop until they had eaten close to the ground when the shepherd would hoe out the roots with a two pronged hoe. The sheep would finish off the roots. In the meantime a new patch of field would have been hurdled off and the sheep would then be moved on. This process continued until the whole field had been cleared. This system of concentrated feeding meant that the land was well manured after the sheep had finished. It would then be plouged and prepared for the next crop, barley, oats or wheat. Today farmers are again resorting to this sort of farming but the question arises, 'is it too late?'. Most of the lovely little field mice have gone, together with many other creatures which inhabited our fields. And there are far fewer wild flowers. At school we were once asked to collect as many specimens of wild flowers as we could and if my memory serves me right I beleive we found nearly eighty different kinds. I doubt if you would match that today on a modern farm.

When barley was grown it was often mixed with clover seed. This grew along with the barley and when it was harvested produced not only barley grain but also a very nourishing kind of cattle feed of barley-straw and clover. The clover crop then continued to grow and the following year would be cut for hay. Then the sheep would be turned into that field during the lambing season and the same pattern would be followed. One special pen was always kept for lambing near to the shepherd's house.

This shepherd's house as it was called was a large hut on wheels; the wheels were always made of iron as wooden ones shrink in hot weather and the hut was out in all weathers. The hut itself was built of good solid timber and was about eighteen feet long by seven wide. It contained a bunk or two, a wood-burning stove and a large cupboard where the shepherd kept all the liniments and medicines for the sheep as well as a small quantity of special food for the weaklings. During the lambing season the shepherd lived in this hut and didn't see much of his family. His wife or children would bring him his main meal daily. The house could be towed to whatever part of the farm it was needed. In wet weather it would require four large horses to pull it, it was so heavy. As far as the shepherd was concerned he must have spent a considerable amount of his life in this house; and remember no over-time, no time off, day after day the same thing. Compared with life today it seems an incredible way of life. But as a boy and in my early teens I saw it and for a while shared in this way of life. I often try and analyse in my own mind how men were able to carry on year after year and never seek a change. Was it because they loved their calling or what it because they just dully accepted that this was their station in life and nothing could alter it?

Another recollection of farm life which stands out very clearly in my memory is the treatment of sick animals. Sometimes a cow would go lame for no apparent reason; the same applied to the sheep. When this happened they would be brought in close to the farm and penned in. A fire would be built and a metal tripod erected over it; from this hung a metal tab of what was called Stockholm tar. When this tar melted each animal would have its cloven hoof filled with it and then be released.

Horses were usually fed on crushed oats and chaff which was cut from hay. Alternatively sometimes after threshing the hulls of corn were used to mix with the feed. When feeding a horse will often blow and snort. Oat hulls were very light and when the horse snorted it would blow the hulls all over the place and often one would get into their eyes. When his happened I remember Father used to have a length of pipe about the thickness of a pencil; a small quantity of sugar would be poured into this pipe and one man would hold the horse steady while another blew this mixture into the affected eye. It certainly effected a cure.

At the time of which I write there was important industry in Dorchester, at Fordington, where Eddison built his great engines for steam-rolling on the roads, and the great steam-ploughs which operated on the surrounding hills. Two of these ploughs were used, one stationed at each side of the field to be ploughed. In addition to their propellant power they had great revolving drums underneath; around these drums was a very stout steel cable which was attached to a large twelve furrowed plough, six of the shares facing one way and six the other. When one set of shares was ploughing the other six were tilted up and were controlled by a man seated high up in the centre. These ploughs were used extensively until the advent of the tractor during the First World War.

Now the greatest problem with these engines was the prodigious amount of coal and water which they used. When they were working they kept two teams of horses and two carters fully occupied all day carting coal and water to feed these giants. The water tank, a huge thing on four wheels, probably held several hundred gallons; this had to be filled by pumping the water from the well by hand. The coal had to be brought from the station, loaded from the railway truck into the carts by hand and then unloaded the same say. There was no time to spare for the poor fellows; as soon as the driver of the engine noticed his water getting low he would start to whistle for water and could be heard a mile away. In bad weather this was a particularly difficult job because the ground was so churned up where the great wheels of the engine had passed. If it rained it became a quagmire and I have seen as many as four great shire horses straining to pull a wagon loaded with Welsh steam coal through this to reach the engine. The same difficulties were experienced with the water tank.

I remember hearing a story at that time when there had been a meeting of farmers discussing the future of the steam-plough. Some were recommending that they invest in them and one farmer is reputed to have said that he would only consider doing so if he had a coal mine at one end of his farm and the sea at the other.

So much for the steam-plough. The steam-rollers were very popular though and gave employment to a great many men.

The other principal industry in Dorchester was the brewery, Eldridge and Pope. Happily this is still a flourishing business today. I am happy to have met Mr Christopher Pope the present joint managing director of the company. He took a considerable interest in my first little booklet about life at Bushes Bottom because he remembers it as a boy in the way I have described it.

My father once had a mishap when loading coal for the steam-ploughs. A large lump of coal fell on to his hand splitting open his little finger. There was no such thing as first aid equipment on farms in those days and so his finger became septic. Father decided that he had better let the doctor see it but on his way had to pass through a gypsy encampment. One of the old ladies enquired what was wrong with his hand and he showed her. She said 'I can cure that' and picked a marshmallow leaf which she steeped in boiling water and placed on the wound stating 'the rough side to draw, the smooth to heal'. Father went on to the doctor, told him what was wrong and what the gypsy had recommended and the doctor agreed that it was as good treatment as any he could give. Sure enough in a few days the finger healed up and ever after that I know that the marshmallow plant was a must in our garden.

Of course today the story of the Tolpuddle Martyrs is known throughout the world but at the time of which I write the memory of this was still fresh in the minds of the older generation and had been passed from father to son. Fortunately by the time I was a child things had improved in the way of wages and so on. The weekly wage had risen from nine to sixteen shillings a week. The way of life was slowly improving and farmers like Henry Duke showed some consideration for the men who worked for him. My father was happy working for him and looking back at the conditions prevailing in the country districts of Dorset, in spite of the long hours and the isolation of living where we did, our lot was far better than in many surrounding areas. I suppose that I was very lucky to have escaped the kind of life which many of my school friends endured. I often wonder what would have happened if Henry had not died at the early age of fifty nine. I am sure that my father would have remained at Bushes. By that time my brother had left school and was already working on the farm and I suppose that there would have been no alternative for me. But it is strange how certain events change the course of one's life. I know that when Henry Duke died my father was shattered and I remember my parents talking about the future and my mother saying, 'well, if we move let's make it a good one'. There is no doubt whatever that this event did change the course of my life.

One of the things which had made me feel rather sad on my recent visits to Godmanstone churchyard is that I have found Henry Duke's grave to be so neglected. After all he laid the foundation for a great business future for his descendants and it seems a shame that he is apparently forgotten.

At harvest time men would do overtime and work till dusk; for this they had the choice of sixpence or their tea. Needless to say most men chose the sixpence. When you think that men were working seven days a week for so little it seems hardly possible that such vast changes have taken place in one lifetime.

I doubt if people living in these circumstances ever knew the meaning of real happiness, certainly not of ease. Life was so hard and if you lived in the country you were bound to the soil, there was no possibility of escape. Perhaps a young man might occasionally have broken away and joined the army or the navy but the opportunity to do this was very limited. You will hear people ask today why people had such large families if they were so poor. There were probably two reasons. First was ignorance and secondly a large family gave the parents a sense of security for their old age. One of the greatest fears people had in those days was of ending up in the workhouse if they became ill or unable to care for themselves after they were too old to work.

Unless they had family who looked after them they were moved into the workhouse. Wives went to one part of the building and husbands to another and in most cases they never saw each other again before they died. Today it seems almost unbelievable that such conditions ever existed but they did, and in my lifetime. The misery and unhappiness that must have been endured by those poor people after a life of hardship hardly bears thinking about.

If you visit Cerne Abbas and go to view the giant you may see on the hil behind you a great gaunt building which was the workhouse. I never pass it without thinking of the misery endured there. There was another at Charminster when I was a boy and when we went to school in Godmanstone it was an everyday sight to see one or more tramps as they were called slowly walking through the village. If you had nowhere to live and no dependents you could move from one workhouse to another. In order to pay for the night's accommodation you had to do two hours work in the morning before leaving, such as chopping wood, gardening or any other task the workhouse master required. Having done this you were sent on your way until you reached the next workhouse in the evening and repeated the performance.

CHAPTER SEVEN

Going to School

The restrictions on age for commencing school in those days, at least in the village, were very relaxed. I started at three years old. I remember very little of the earliest days except that I was taken by my eldest sister and looked after by her while there.

Nearly all the children attending these village schools came from poor families; most of the men in the villages worked on the land. Some were shepherds, some cowmen or carters, the others who would today be classified as labourers, were known as strappers; they did the hedging, ditching, fencing and hoeing, etc. Wages for a farm labourer at the time we lived in Martinstown were sixteen shillings a week.

In my earliest memories of school life I seem to remember that girls usually wore frilly pinafores in class and boys knickerbockers, buttoning just below the knee, a Norfolk type jacket, heavy hobnail boots and, in wet weather, leather button-up leggings. Girls' footwear was boots which came half way up the calf and buttoned at the side. Today these clothes are museum pieces.

Our journey to school from Bushes Bottom was a very hard one. First we had to climb Crete Hill; in those days it was all chalk and in wet or frosty weather was very slippery. Having reached the summit there was the long trek down the other side. This was a tiring journey for a five year old and the thought of it today makes me shudder but I suppose we knew no other means of transport except Shanks's pony so just accepted it. It meant an early rise every morning as we had to leave at eight. We had to be in the playground by ten minutes to nine or suffer the wrath of the headmistress.

Godmanstone school was small but well attended. I should think there were upwards of sixty children who came from Nethercerne, Forston Bushes and Godmanstone itself. There were two full time teachers, Miss Hoare was the Head and Miss Durden her assistant. Incidentally her mother, Mrs Durden ran the little general shop. Then a senior girl, Kathleen Lee, assisted with the infants. There were no facilities available for children who lived too far away to go home for dinner so we always brought a large can of cocoa to school and sandwiches or suchlike. In cold weather we were allowed to stand the can on the tortoise stove to warm but at twelve o'clock we were turned out regardless of the weather, so we used to seek refuge in Farmer Fowler's wagon shed and sit on the shafts of the wagon and eat our meal.

The education provided was very basic, little more than the three Rs. One thing we were never allowed to forget, however, was that we were subjects of an empire on which the sun never set.

One of my earliest memories of doing anything at school

was of rag picking. This consisted of being given a piece of material and then pulling it to pieces, thread by thread, until you had a ball of wadding. These balls were sent to various engineering establishments and used by the engine drivers to wipe their hands on and to clean the brass works on the engines. At that particular time steam-engines were used extensively for ploughing, threshing machines and steam-rolling the roads.

I do remember one question put to the school by the Headmistress: 'If I had a sum of money and I spent part of it what should I have?'. Each child was asked in turn. Many had answers but all were wrong and the teacher became exasperated and said, 'I will give two pence to the child who can give me the right answer'. I had been thinking about it and could only see one answer so raised my hand; she said 'Well, what would I have?' and I said, 'You would have less'. Reluctantly she gave me the two pence and later in the afternoon when I must have done something to displease her she expressed regret at having done so. But that is how things were.

Another memory is quite vivid. My pal George Budden and I had been up in the wagon shed during dinner time and on our return to school we found the door open and the key, which was a large heavy one, lying on the floor in two pieces. George picked it up and we both looked at it in astonishment but before we could go in search of anyone Miss Hoare, the headmistress, appeared and declared that she had caught us red-handed. We were accused of breaking the key and were kept in at playtime and after school for about two weeks to make us own up. Needless to say we could not do that as we had not broken it but only after the vicar was called in and we swore on the Bible that we had no knowledge of how it was broken were we at last believed. George and I had our own ideas as to how that key was broken; the headmistress always locked the door at dinner time and therefore must have unlocked it, but we kept these conclusions to ourselves. This memory came back as clearly as it it had been yesterday instead of seventy years before.

Sport had never been introduced into village schools in those days. On rare occasions in spring and summer we would be taken on a nature study ramble along the hedgerows and in the woods; apart from this, school provided a limited education.

Most village schools were Church of England schools; the governors were the local vicar, the lord of the manor and probably one other local person who was sufficiently well off to make a donation to the church, and the head teacher. When Christmas came there was usually a school concert followed by a tea party; medals and certificates were awarded for good attendance. Obviously in a village like Godmanstone where so many children had to walk great distances to school these awards always went to the children who actually lived in the village. No child from Bushes Bottom ever received one. Prizegiving was rounded off by a song, always the same song; this was *Hearts of Oak* sung with great gusto. By the time I left school I knew it off by heart.

The party was always popular. We had bread and butter and cakes and after the festivities had ended we all had to line up and file out of the school room, as we left we were given an apple and an orange. All this was provided by the lord of the manor.

There was also always a harvest festival, or, as it was called a harvest home. This was held in the barn at Manor Farm. The old barn is still there although the last time I passed it I noticed that the big double doors facing the road were hanging off. I hope that someone will take steps to preserve it, for so much of local history is invested in that building. It was always used for elections, coronations, and any other gatherings which took place.

We always had two days' holiday at Whitsun, two weeks at Christmas, two weeks and Easter, and the month of August. There was a half day on 24 May, that being Empire Day. The morning was spent looking at a map of the world and listening to the headmistress and the vicar expound the glories of the greatest empire the world had ever known, covering one fifth of the world's surface, and a quarter of the population. An empire on which the sun never set.

As children we were very proud of this; poor and uneducated as we were, we had grown up to believe that we were invincible as a nation. So at the outbreak of the First World War young men of military age, believing this, rushed to join up. What we didn't know was that like a great old tree the trunk was rotten and when the storm came it was blown over. I heard that in losing Lord Kitchener we lost our one great military leader whom no one could replace. As history has recorded, the break up of the British Empire commenced with the battle of the Somme in 1916, which showed up with disastrous clarity the ineptitide of the high command. This is recorded in detail, but I remember it, I met and talked to boys I went to school with who had fought in that battle, and heard first hand the mistakes which had been made.

A pleasant memory of that school was the Annual Outing to Weymouth every summer. Everyone went on this outing, parents and school dignitaries, namely Mr Smith, Rev. Pope, Mr Bailey and one other whose name escapes me. The outing started at seven in the morning when we all piled into the farm wagons, the horses with their harness cleaned and polished, topknots and bells on their heads. To the best of my recollection the journey took about three hours. Nowadays the trip to New York can be done in the time it took us to go to and from Weymouth.

On arrival our first visit was to the penny bazaar where a pail and shovel were purchased for one penny. Then my mother would pop round to see her Uncle Pearce who was at that time Weymouth's Town Crier. Then on to the beach. I used to be fascinated watching the horses pulling the bathing huts down as the tide went out and pulling them in again as it turned. But we had a good time with a dig in the sand, a donkey ride and a penny ice cream cornet, and returned home tired but happy.

At this time of year the horse coaches used to run from Sherborne to Weymouth and return through the village at about five-thirty. This usually happened on a Thursday, so we used to walk along the road towards Forston and wait for them; when the occupants saw children waving they would throw out pennies. This led to a terrible tragedy. We had walked along the road and were more than half-way to Forston when we saw the first of the coaches coming. We all waited excitedly, but as the coach reached us one little girl ran forward, tripped and fell under the horses' hooves and was killed instantly. Her name was Betty Cheesman and she lived at Forston. After this we were forbidden ever again to follow this practice.

On the Saturday following the whole school went to see this little girl as she lay in her coffin. I have never forgotten that pale serene little face.

During the five-and-a-half years that I attended school at Godmanstone I never remember a medical officer coming to the school, or an attendance officer. I do know however that when we moved to the Isle of Wight a medical officer attended once a year. The standards of hygiene were almost non-existent. In Godmanstone the toilets were housed in a little long building which, incidentally, is still there; there were two for the boys and two for the girls, bucket type. It was the caretaker's job to empty them. There were no washing facilities whatever, no wash basins or towels, no water even. The same state of affairs prevailed in most homes where the toilet was usually a little hut at the bottom of the garden, twenty yards or so from the house. They were almost always the bucket type, although in some cases it was a cess pit and again hardly any cottages had a tap indoors. I know that conditions in towns were different; when we visited my grandma in Dorchester I remember being shown how to pull the chain of the toilet and the noise it made used to frighten me to death.

I remember that the most dreaded disease prevalent among the schoolchildren was diphtheria. If a child contracted this it was almost always fatal. Scarlet fever was also very common and if a case of chickenpox or measles broke out the school would be closed for six weeks. Another disease much dreaded was consumption or T.B. This was more common in teenagers and adults than in children and again in those days was usually fatal. Fortunately these diseases have almost been wiped out nowadays but when I was a boy they were a very real and constant source of worry for parents, although I suppose that progress was being made medically.

In spite of all the hardships and discomforts I never remember any of our family being ill; a common cold now and again but I don't recall anyone being laid up for sickness of any sort. I often wonder why. Perhaps we lived in such a remote place that it was free from germs or perhaps the way of living and the type of food were in fact quite healthy.

One noticeable thing today is that when I visit villages like Martinstown I miss the sound of schoolchildren at play. Many schools have closed and no doubt the children are transported to a much more modern type of school where they enjoy greater educational opportunities then my generation did but I still remember the sounds of playtime, the laughter, the squealing and shouting; the following lines say it all;

There was no time to eat our tea
Or go indoors to wait and see
People change, but children never
I wish I could have been a child for ever.

CHAPTER 8

Godmanstone Village

This little village has hardly changed since the time I write about. I notice that the farm on the right hand side of the road going north is no longer occupied and seems derelict. At this farm lived Mr Smith and his family during the period I was at Bushes. He was Henry Duke's farm manager and came on horseback to Bushes Bottom every Sunday morning to give orders for the week ahead. The stables at his house housed two teams of shires and several hunters. He had two sons, Hector and Walter, who attended school in the village. I remember Walter falling and breaking his arm on two occasions. This again was a job for Dr Dalton, no going off to hospital, as today.

I remember the little general store and sweet shop which was one of the last houses on the right hand side of the road going towards Cerne Abbas. Then came the Smith's Arms which is still there; in those days it did not enjoy the popularity it does today. Then came the Post Office, the postmaster was Mr Crabb. I incurred his displeasure on one occasion when I filled the pillar box with grass. A little stream ran behind his house with a wooden bridge crossing it and in the garden were some fine plum trees which overhung the stream. Many is the time that I, together with other children, have waded into this stream to collect the fallen fruit.

A little further along after one or two more houses was the Vicarage. The Rev Pope resided here, a tall bald-headed man, who looked disagreeable but that belied his true nature for he was kind. I know that after my accident he used to walk over the hill to visit me and see how I was. Then on the opposite side of the road past the school was Fowler's Farm. We always knew it as that because it was occupied by a Mr Fowler; his barn ran alongside the road and at the end of the barn was the blacksmith's shop. I believe the blacksmith's name was Mr Bolham. I went there many times with my father when he took the horses for shoeing. At that time the blacksmith was a very busy man as all the horses in the area came there. His shop is still there; two years ago I found the doors open and had a look inside and there was the anvil and water trough in which he cooled the red hot iron. The old fireplace where he heated the iron was there but the bellows had been removed and dumped in a corner. On the wall stretching right to the apex of the building are the pegs where the smith used to hang sets of shoes for his customers' horses; as a boy I remember that each peg was named for the horse whose shoes hung there.

Beyond this, going towards Forston, was a small group of houses on the left. I remember the names of some of the occupants, there was Mr Cutler and family, the Hawkins family - Reg Hawkins was one of the boys who won a medal for attendance at school every year - the Selbys, Mr Selby and his sons where the shepherds for Henry Duke. Another young couple was Bob and Betty Grant. It was from Bob that my young sister got her pet black and white rabbit, later to be devoured by foxes. Then a little further on lived the Frys. I don't remember much about this family except that they seemed to be quite well off. I know that at the outbreak of the war rumours went round that they were being interned. I never knew the truth of it all and only know that in those very early days they had a wireless aerial on the house.

Back to the school where our play area was in fact the road leading to the church. This was a charming little church surrounded by trees on the village side, while at the back and on one side the fields stretched away up over Crete Hill. To leave Godmanstone to get home we had to turn right after leaving school, go through a gate and past Fowler's Farm and away up the hill.

The harvest home was always held in Fowler's Barn when all the village came to feast and dance. It was also used on the occasion of King George V's coronation celebrations. An incident occurred on this occasion worthy of mention. As children we used to eat our dinner in Fowler's wagon shed sitting on the shafts of the wagons. On the day when the celebrations were to take place the barn had been decorated with flags and bunting and the tables laid out ready for the evening. In addition to this a very large cask of beer had been set up on a stand and tapped ready for use. Now, as children we were curious to see inside the barn and it so happened that poor Harry Budden had been brought over from Bushes to keep the place tidy. Well, some of the older boys asked Harry if he would like a drink. Harry said he would, so he was persuaded to lie on his back with his mouth open under the tap of the beer barrel, the tap was turned on and in a short space of time Harry was shouting and rolling about in the beer. The noise brought Mr Fowler to see what was happening. We ran and he turned off the tap and came roaring into school telling the teachers what had happened and asking them to sort out those responsible. They owned up and were duly punished. That night along the top of Crete and Cowden Hills great bonfires were lit, great ricks of gorse had been built weeks before and had dried out; they created a blaze that could be seen for miles.

On the right hand side of the lane leading to the church was a high stone wall which enclosed a large house and garden. I believe that at one time Henry Duke lived in this house and have a feeling that he died there, but am not sure. I do know however that when he died his lovely hunter which he had ridden to hounds up to the time of his death was turned out to roam with the cattle at Bushes Bottom. It was a fine blue roan and year after I remember my father recounting the following story about that horse.

When the war broke out in 1914 the army came looking for horses, chose this one and asked my father to deliver it to Dorchester Artillery Barracks the following Sunday morning. Well now, this horse had been running wild for a year and was very difficult to handle. But father was a good horseman and eventually gained control of him and rode off to Dorchester. On arrival the officer in charge examined the horse and realised that it was a bit wild so he asked father if he would wait until the young officer who was to take charge of this horse was ready as he was a bit nervous. Father agreed but it was quite some time before this officer appeared. In the meantime the horse had got cold and when the officer prepared to mount the horse just went wild, reared up and fell backwards and broke his neck; and that was the end of that. But it was a lovely creature. I have often thought since that in view of the suffering endured by horses in the war it was better that it went that way.

The school lane came after Mr Duke's house. There are two cottages in the lane; the Downtons lived in one, he was the gardener for Henry Duke, and in the other lived the handyman who cleaned the school and drove Henry Duke's car.

CHAPTER NINE
School Holidays

In the days of which I write there were no half-term holidays; we had two weeks at Easter, the month of August and two weeks at Christmas. In addition to this were two days at Whitsum and a half-day holiday on Empire Day. As a family we never went away for a holiday, one reason being that farm workers were never given holidays, and the second being that there was no money for such things. So we used to walk to Winterbourne Abbas to see my maternal grandmother and aunt and perhaps spend a night there; it was a pretty good walk from Bushes Bottom, about six miles each way, as anyone who knows that district will appreciate.

The other outing was to see my other grandmother in Dorchester. She was an invalid and couldn't walk and was cared for by my aunt, my father's youngest sister. Apart from these outings the holidays were spent in the valley.

During the Easter holiday the great potato planting took place. Mr Duke used to set aside a field for this and all the employees in the district were given a day off to plant a row of potatoes right across a field. This was usually some distance from our farmstead, over the hill towards Sydling, but all the families took part.

The furrow was opened by a kind of double-furrowed plough drawn by one horse throwing the soil to each side and leaving a nice deep trench for planting. Our job was to place the potatoes in this furrow, properly spaced. Then the plough, or Bock as it was called, was driven up between the rows. This had the effect not only of covering the potatoes but also of hoeing them up at the same time; consequently they needed no further attention until they were harvested. This happened in the autumn, always on a Saturday when the children were home from school. The same implement was used to plough the potatoes out. Our job was to pick them up and fill the sacks. A fire was started with all the dead haulm and hedge trimmings and when this had been completed large potatoes were pushed into the embers to bake; after the carts were loaded and we wended our way home eating hot baked potatoes.

During the holidays we children were allocated certain duties. One of these was to gather fir and pine cones from the wood down the valley. These were put into sacks which were collected by horse and cart as was all the wood that was collected. Sometimes we would find trees which had blown down, then we would tell our parents and the men came with a large cross-saw to cut them up. We could then carry the pieces to the edge of the wood where they would be picked up by the horse and cart and taken home to be stored for the winter.

A great deal of gorse was cut in the summer and bundled and left to dry for winter fuel. There were acres of gorse and patches would be burnt in rotation; the men then shared out the sticks for firewood and made faggots out of that to put into the bread oven. The families had no rights to cut wood, but could take fallen timber.

Further up the valley there was a bed of hazels. The gypsies used to collect wood there. The women made clothes pegs from young straight stalks of hazel which they bound at the tops with strips of metal cut from old tins which they collected. And very clever they were at it. They went round selling these pegs. Of course they were not averse to a bit of poaching even in those days. I remember seeing their ponies which were always unharnessed and followed along behind the caravans like dogs. It was a very picturesque sight to see them on the move in their brightly coloured caravans, drawn by horses, and a number of loose ponies trailing along behind. These always appeared to be well cared for as did the children. It is so different today when they travel in big lorries with very expensive caravans behind and spend their time collecting old iron and scrap.

Another of our pastimes was rabbiting. We used to cut a very large bramble from the bushes, trim all the prickles from one end to enable us to hold it comfortably and then proceed to the rabbit warren; the idea was to push this bramble into a rabbit hole and, if you touched a rabbit, twist it round and round hoping to get the prickly end entangled in the rabbit's fur and so be able to pull it out. Needless to say this was never successful in our case but these excursions did have one amazing result. One day we were up on Magiston hill, three of us, my brother and my friend George and myself and we each had our brambles pushed into a hole of a large warren and were sitting waiting. I was spreading the fresh soil which had been thrown out by the rabbits' digging and noticed what appeared to be two tiny silver balls. I pulled them out of the soil and it was a tiny purse. I opened it and behold, inside were five gold sovereigns. I can remember it vividly to this day. I couldn't believe my eyes. The brambles were left in the holes and we ran home. My mother was astonished but decided that the purse and money should be put aside until Mr Smith came on Sunday. When he came father took the purse and its contents out to him and explaned how we had come by it. Mr Smith was of the opinion that it had been lost by one of the lady huntswomen who rode with the hounds the previous winter and I remember his comment to my father: 'I think that you can do more good with it George than the person who lost it.' So we all had new clothes and boots to go back to school with after that holiday.

During the Easter holidays we would walk miles birds' nesting. In those days we used to collect the eggs and blow them and put them in a case of cottol wool. One had to be careful not to take more than one egg from each nest. The eggs were then labelled and it is surprising what a collection could be built up. Of course this has been illegal for a long time now and very necessarily or there would be few birds left.

Our other recreations were tree climbing and swinging on an old rope swing we had fixed up on the bough of a large ash tree. Another pastime we enjoyed was climbing to the top of the straw in the barn and sliding down; this was great fun.

During August, harvesting was well under way so we used to go to the harvest field where they were cutting the corn and follow the binder as often as it went round. Rabbits would run out and we would endeavour to catch them. We called the, then modern, reaper a binder, as it tied the corn into sheaves and threw them out ready to be stacked for drying. The days of mowing by hand had passed and the only mowing that was done was when they opened up a field for the binder to get to start work. This binder was drawn by three horses unless it was a particularly steep field when a fourth would be used in front of the other three; a boy was needed to ride this horse. I have done it many times.

The days of gleaning had also ended. After all the stacks had been picked up if there seemed to be a lot of loose corn and straw it would be horse-raked and picked up and fed to the cattle.

I remember on one occasion my mother sent me and my second eldest sister on an errand to Sydling. We set out to walk over the hill and when we had reached a rather remote spot about halfway there we went through a gate and came face to face with two badgers. We turned and ran, and never got to Sydling. Mother said that she expected the badgers did the same.

On another occasion my companion and I were walking up the valley and had gone further than we normally did. We came across the ruins of an old house. Well, it could hardly be described as ruins as only the foundations were left but the garden remained still. It was all overgrown but in one corner was a large apple tree loaded with lovely red apples. We filled our pockets after sampling them.

When we got home of course everyone wanted to know where the apples came from, so the next day being Sunday, we guided the menfolk to this tree and the apples were quickly picked and shared.

Another incident which stands out in my memory is the day when we wandered some way from home over the hill towards Sydling and, on climbing a slight rise in the ground, we came face to face with a large Red Devon steer pawing the ground and bellowing; as soon as he saw us he made for us. Close by was a very large patch of gorse and in the hot weather the sheep used to tunnel into the bushes for shelter from the sun. We dived into one of these and crawled in as far as we could. The steer went charging past and we spent the next couple of hours sitting in there hoping that it had gone. Eventally we came out, saw no trace of the herd and ran home. When I told my father what had happened he warned us to keep well away from cattle on hot days as often the heat and flies upset them and made them bad-tempered.

From these brief experiences the reader will gain some idea of the wildness of that valley in those days. In the normal way we were never afraid of animals.

The winter holiday was the worst at Bushes. If the weather was bad we could play in the barn or fall back on the old-fashioned indoor games. Of course there was no radio or any type of music available, except the mouth organ which I played, but this did not go down too well with listeners while I was learning to play.

Gathering holly and the like for Christmas decorations we enjoyed; there were no other decorations such as we have today. I remember a boy at school being given an electric torch for Christmas and how we all crowded round in the darkest corner of a barn to see how it worked.

One interesting job that used to take place in the winter evenings was making rabbit snares. This my brother and father did and I was never tired of watching them. They would have three strands of thin copper wire which they would double, leaving a loop at one end. Through this loop was passed a rod; onto the other end of the wire a flat iron was tied. This was spun round many times until the wire had been twisted into a strong six-stranded wire. The flat iron was then removed. The end of the wire was then passed through a loop thus making a wire noose. A cord was then made fast to the wire at one end, the other end of the cord was fastened to a peg about a foot long and when the trap was set for the rabbit this peg would be firmly driven into the ground. The noose would be set up on a split stick in a regular rabbit run and when the rabbit ran its head went through the noose and that was the end.

Another method for catching rabbits employed by the men in the valley was the use of a long-net. This was about one hundred yards long and was taken out by the men on a moonlit evening and set up along a hedge by the side of a field or round a rabbit warren. My part in this was to stand at one end of the net with my friend, George, at the other and hold the string which closed the net. When the net began to vibrate strongly we knew that it contained one or more rabbits. We would then give a shout and the men would close in and untangle the rabbits and we would then move on to another site.

We were allowed to catch as many rabbits as we liked; there was nothing improper about it. Being situated in such a remote place it was not easy to dispose of any excess so no great effort was made to catch more than were needed from day to day. If my father and brother did catch any extra I used to take them to Mr Gifford who lived in a smallholding at the south end of the valley. He would pay sixpence each for them and take them to Dorchester market with his own dairy produce.

So our holidays were always full of interest and activity. The best part was I suppose that we all joined in and never thought of any other way of life.

I could go on writing about the beauties of that valley. I have tried to paint a word picture of it, but nothing I can say can truly portray it. Only those who lived there or others who saw it could ever appreciate what it was like. But I am afraid that in those days there were so many country places unspoilt by man's search for progress that it was just taken for granted.

Imagine, for instance, walking home from Grimstone station after dark - the sounds of the night, rabbits scuttling away as one approached, perhaps a hedgehog or a fox, the squeal of a rabbit caught by a stoat, and then all along the bank under the hedgerow the glow-worms in their dozens. Yet in this lonely valley walking home after dark aroused no fears such as are experienced today if you walk our streets at night.

As I have said before I am glad that I had the experience of living there at that time and perhaps can convey something of that feeling to anyone who should read this or chance to visit there.

CHAPTER TEN

Dialect of Dorset

I am sure many people today would never understand the old timers if they could hear them talking. I can remember expressions that were used and no doubt used them myself as a boy. Often during a conversation between two people you will hear repeatedly 'you know'; in Dorset this was 'sknow you'. If an enquiry was made as to where an object lying around should be put, the answer would invariably be to 'let n bide where e be too'. If a shepherd or other worker was off to a remote part of the farm he would say 'I must git away up athirt'. A loft over the stables would be known as the 'tollet' and if you should hear men talking after a trip to town you would hear Dorchester pronounced as Dartishter, horses were hosses, and the accent was broad.

I well remember when we moved to the Isle of Wight people with whom we came in contact had great difficulty in understanding us, and although it is now seventy-six years since I lived there people will often say to me 'do you come from the West of England?' to which I reply

'Yes, but I left in 1914'. I think it will be a great pity if these accents die, they are a part of our heritage.

What may seem strange to readers today is that school-teachers never seemed to correct bad pronunciation, it must have been accepted as normal.

Quite recently I sat on the sea-front at Lyme Regis one evening. There were very few people about but three teenage girls were sauntering past talking loudly to each other. I didn't pay any particular attention to their conversation until heard the following said in a loud voice 'my mother told me t'other night'. I realised that nothing much had changed regarding country dialect.

Strange as it may seem if you are born in this environment and grew up in it you never completely lost the accent. I have not lived in Dorset now for seventy years yet people still recognise an accent.

CHAPTER ELEVEN

Changes

I think it was early in 1913 that Mr Henry Duke died and at about that time the Buddens left Bushes and their place was taken by a relation of ours. I knew her as Aunt Amy. The family name had been Rolls but uncle had died and aunt married again. I can't remember her new married name as we always referred to them as the Rolls. They were second cousins to me. There were three boys and three girls. The eldest boy was Ralph, then Leslie, then Frank who was the same age as me so I still had a companion. The girls were Linda, Hilda and Amy and they were all still at school. So now the population of Bushes had been reduced by two.

Ralph was nineteen and the proud owner of a gramophone, so at last we had some alternative entertainment. On summer evenings he would bring it out on to a little grass mound and we would all sit round listening to such songs as 'When Father Papered the Parlour' and 'When Poor Father Joined the Territorials' and many others. It became the practice for each family to contribute to the purchase of a new record occasionally.

By this time my two older sisters had left school and gone into service as was common in those days and my younger sister was not at school.

Of events of national importance of that time I remember the advent of wireless and the arrest of a certain Dr Crippen and his companion as a result of its use. Much was made of this at school and of the future possibilities. Another event was the sinking of the *Titanic* . We had had a lesson at school prior to the sailing of this ship, emphasising that it was unsinkable; then came the news that it had gone down on its first voyage. Here again wireless was used to call for help. Broadcasting to the public did not start till after the war and I well remember a number of the old ladies on whom I called as roundsman were horrified at the idea of listening to it. They used to say that it came from the bottomless pit and steadfastly refused to have anything to do with it.

There is no doubt that wireless, and of course the war, changed the way of life for many in remote districts. They gradually began to make contact with the outside world and learn that they were missing many things in life. I suppose that this may have been one of the main reasons why young men and women left the country districts and sought new life in the towns. And who can blame them?

At that time Dorchester was a great military town. There was an imposing entrance to the barracks of the Dorchester Regiment where the military museum now stands, and the parade ground stretched about two hundred yards along the road to Portland. It was enclosed by tall iron railings but one could stand on the opposite side of the road and watch the soldiers drill.

Back towards the town at the crossroads at the top of the hill stood a large drinking trough where carters and travellers stopped to water their horses. At the bottom of the hill going toward Yeovil a footpath went off to the right along the banks of the Frome to the foot of Friary Hill. To the right of this path was the prison. This was a sinister place to me because we had learned about the Monmouth Rebellion and the trial conducted in Dorchester by Judge Jeffreys. As a boy I used to feel frightened of that place. However just beyond the prison entrance was a restaurant called the Soldier's Home where mother used to take us for a special treat and we did enjoy that.

I remember great posters pasted on the walls at election time. There was a picture of two cottage loaves of bread, one large and one very small with the caption 'Which will you vote for?' I don't know which of the parties exhibited this bill but I do recall the posters.

I remember the Suffragettes. My Uncle Ted came to visit us and told us of how he had pushed some of them to the police station in a wheelbarrow. I heard how one had thrown herself in front the the King's horse at the Derby in 1913 and was killed.

I have so often thought of our last summer at Bushes Bottom in 1914. My brother had left school and although life seemed to go on the same there were distant rumblings that I heard the adults talking of. But they seemed so far away, as if they couldn't affect us.

It was that summer that I saw my first aeroplane. It flew over the valley towards Cerne Abbas.

My brother used to keep pigeons and he had four carriers. That summer the police came and took them away saying that they would be returned if all went well. They never came back.

August came and with it the school holidays. We spent our time as usual in the harvest fields. Despite rumours of war we went happily on our way as usual. Then one day father came home with a newspaper. War had been declared on Germany. I can still vividly remember my father reading Sir Edward Grey's words 'The lights of Europe are going out, we shall not see them relit in our time'. These words made a deep impression on me and I have never forgotten them.

My cousins Ralph and Leslie went off and volunteered for military service. They both passed A1; two or three weeks later they were called up. I never saw them again. Ralph was killed at Gallipoli while landing at Suvla Bay on 25 April 1915. What a long time ago and yet his memory remains so fresh. I was very fond of Ralph, I suppose one could describe it as hero worship; he was so tall and strong and always laughing and cheerful. It seemed so unreal that any young man could go from such a peaceful beautiful valley and die a violent death in a foreign land.

Things went on much the same in the valley, the birds sang and the sum shone continuously. It was a lovely summer. We followed the binder, carried beer to the harvesters, but there was no denying that a shadow hung over all. Then it was time to return to school. The holiday was over but little was I to know that that was to be my last summer at Bushes Bottom.

The Saturday following our return to school my father went to Dorchester. There he met by chance a well-known farmer from Broadmayne, a Mr Alfy Coleman. He offered father a good job if he would accompany his son to the Isle of Wight where he had bought him a farm. He wanted someone he knew and could trust to go with him. He agreed to pay all expenses. So after it had been duly considered it was agreed that we should go and when Mr Smith came as usual on Sunday morning father told him of his decision. It was agreed that we should leave on 11 October.

The next month was a month of preparation for us. As the days passed we went to see our grandmothers and aunts to say goodbye. On the morning of 11 October 1914 we said goodbye to our friends and to Bushes Bottom.

Mr Coleman's wagon and horses arrived for our furniture. This was loaded and went off to Broadmayne where another wagon had been loaded for a second family, who were also going, together with a wagon loaded with food for the horses and cattle that were going. They all travelled by road from Broadmayne to Lymington and then by boat over to the island and thence on to Calbourne.

My mother, young sister and I stayed in Dorchester with an aunt until we heard from father that they had arrived and settled in. We had a most interesting week in Dorchester with my aunt, uncle and cousins. At that time the war had been raging for over two months and German prisoners of war were arriving and being housed temporarily in the artillery barracks. My cousin Jack and I spent many hours watching the recruiting sergeant drilling a squad of men on the parade ground and now and again he would come to the railings and appeal for volunteers. This always met with a satisfactory response from the young men watching. I have often wondered since that time how many of those whom I watched go through that gateway survived.

During that week we also had a good time playing along the river bank and I recall one occasion when we had climbed a tree overhanging the river, started larking about and finally fell into the river. Fortunately it was not deep at that point so all we suffered was a good soaking and arrived home in a pretty bedraggled state.

We then heard from father that all was ready for us in our new home in Calbourne so the great journey, as it was to us in those days, began. I can still remember the thrill of that train and boat journey to children like us who had led such a quiet life in remote country districts. It is difficult to convey our excitement.

We boarded the ferry at Lymington and crossed to Yarmouth. In those days ferries were paddle boats and all goods traffic was towed behind in big black barges. On arrival at Yarmouth we had about half a mile to walk to the station where there was a single track line which ran from Freshwater to Newport. This served the western end of the island. I well remember our surprise when we boarded this train because the seats had no cushions, they were just bare polished wood and the train seemed to go so slowly after the Great Western. After two stops we arrived at Calbourne and found we had another walk of one-and-a-half miles to reach our new abode. But here we had good roads leading right to the house where we were to live. Opposite our house across the road was a great park surrounded by a double row of beech trees and away to the right could be seen a large white house. The constant call of peacocks filled the air as they roamed the park.

CHAPTER TWELVE

Return to Dorset

After this great move I spent the remainder of my boyhood in the Isle of Wight. On leaving school I worked for two years on a farm but was very keen not to be bound to the land and moved into the bakery trade. I spent the rest of my working life in that trade. As a young man I moved to London and lived there and in the South East for many years, moving to the Midlands some time after the end of the Second World War. It was never possible to return to Dorset.

In 1983 I was at last able to return to this part of Dorset. One of my deepest regrets is that I had lost my life's partner three years earlier. I would dearly have loved to have had her with me on my return, particularly as her grandparents were Wessex people. For fifteen years before her death she had been an invalid and that made the journey impossible.

But I am fortunate in having sons and a daughter who look after me and grandchildren and great-grandchildren; so what more can one ask? When I did return I came with my daughter and two grandsons. I first arrived at the little farm which had been the Gifford's smallholding and found it in a wonderful state of preservation. It had obviously been well cared for. The only thing missing as far as I could see was the honeysuckle over the front porch, but I had a feeling that it was no longer a smallholding, everything looked so clean and there was no sign of any animals or chickens.

I enquired from a young man mixing cement if the bridle path to Bushes Bottom still existed. With a curious look he told me that it did and then his curiousity got the better of him and he asked me why I was interested. When I told him that I used to live there he became quite enthusiastic. I commented on the little farmhouse and mentioned the Giffords and he told me that Mr Gifford still lived in a house opposite standing well back from the lane. So I decided to go and see him.

I walked up through the garden and was struck by the signs of decay and neglect everywhere. When I knocked on the door a thin pale man with a slight straggly beard answered. I introduced myself and explained that I had known the Giffords year ago. It turned out that he was the grandson of the Mr Gifford I had known and the two boys who emigrated to Canada were his uncles. He told me that both had returned during the First World War serving in the Canadian army, both had survived and had returned to Canada.

We then set out to walk to Bushes and reached the edge of the wood, but it had all changed; there were no fir trees and the woood seemed to be very thin. In the days I remembered it was very dark inside and at least twice the size. However we could not get through as there was corn growing in the field where the path once ran, so we went up the hill a little way until we could just see the large trees at Bushes Bottom. When my grandsons who were with me saw where I wanted to go they backed out. There was no way I was going to persuade them to walk up that valley. But I noticed that the lovely hedge which had extended up the valley had gone and been replaced by a wire fence. Also all the gorse, bushes, and trees were gone and as far as eye could see there was golden corn. As we walked back past the Giffords' house the day on which we had left came back to me so clearly. As we were on our way to Grimstone station the Giffords came out to say goodbye and wish us well.

Then on to Godmanstone to try and retrace my steps of long ago; but so much has changed. No longer can you walk along the village street and hear the ring of the blacksmith's hammer on the anvil, or the clop clop of the carrier's horse trotting homeward, the common sounds of my childhood. No longer do clouds of dust rise as a car passes. I wandered up the lane to the building which had been our school. The door was open and I went inside and the memories came flooding back, girls and boys who had been at schoold with me and I wondered where they all were not. I wandered into the infants' room which seemed so small now and then stood in the porch and gazed at the big old door.

I went on up the lane into the churchyard where I searched for the names of those who had gone. I came to the graves of Henry Duke and his wife and remembered my parents' grief at his passing. In the lovely little church I noticed on the war memorial plaque four names and again my feelings were stirred by seeing the name Ernest Ralph Rolls and remembering all the good times we had together.

Going back slowly down the lane by the high stone wall I noticed the climbing plant with tiny blue flowers which still grew there and remembered how a number of the bigger boys had once received a severe caning for pulling pieces off. I recalled the people who had lived in the cottages. I reached the main road and right opposite is the house which used to be the Post Office but is so no longer; and I remembered George Crabb the postmaster and his little boy Tim and the time when he chased me for stuffing the pillar box full of grass.

I wandered across the road to the Smith's Arms, now very busy and obviously a tourist attraction. I stood on the bank of the stream which runs along the rear of the pub and the house that was the post office and, as I gazed into the water which ran slowly by, it seemed to be reminding me of all the details of long ago when as children we paddled in this stream and collected the plums which had fallen into the water. I looked across the little wooden bridge to the fields and hedgerows where we were sometimes taken for nature-study walks. Still the water flows on reminding me that this stream had provided the power for the mill at Nethercerne which was owned and run by the father of two of my schoolfriends, Reg and Bert Baker. I clearly remember their father driving through the village regularly with the wagon loaded with flour. Now no trace of the mill remains, it has been swept away by the passage of time.

However I did succeed in tracing Bert Baker, when I returned in 1983. He now lives at Piddlehinton. I called to see him and we had a long talk about the old days, remembering how his brother Reg, who was now dead, had got the cane nearly every day at school and how his mother used to go to tell the teacher what she thought of her - to no avail for the teacher was a hard taskmaster and the slightest thing was made an excuse for using the cane. I heard from him that the mill no longer existed and that he had worked on the land all his life and never married. When I called to see him a year later I found the windows boarded up and the garden overgrown so imagine that he too has passed on.

Over the road and through the gate up the track we trod so many times as children to Manor Farm, now run by Will Best. Peeping into the yard I see still standing the old barn where the harvest home and never-to-be-forgotten coronation celebrations were held. The wagon shed is there, used now for much more modern equipment than it housed seventy years ago. I stood and looked up the track to the top of Crete Hill where a group of tall trees still stand and remembered how as a boy I would pick a bunch of daffodils there in the spring; the ground was covered with them in among the trees. I longed to be able to retrace my steps of the past up the track. About half way up there is a lovely wood on the right where we listened to the pigeons cooing. George and I would loiter on our way home from school. On the left of the track was a thick hedge and once we found a robin's nest there built in an old kettle, and watched it daily till the eggs were hatched and the little ones flew. As I stood there I could remember my father taking his wagon laden with wattled hurdles up the hill, drawn by three cart horses. When they reached the top, before starting the descent down the other side, what were known as drag shoes were put under the rear wheels of the wagon to hold it back. It was so steep no horse could ever have done so. I always felt that one of the most majestic sights on a farm was a team of three or four great cart horses straining to pull a heavy load. The stength of these animals was a sight never to be forgotten; but such scenes will not be repeated.

I went back down to the road to the village. The forge is still there but most of the other cottages have gone and in their place are pretty little bungalows. As I drove along the road towards Dorchester I passed the spot where little Betty Cheesman died so tragically all those years ago, and realised that the last time I had stood on this ground was when as children we had gone to say our last goodbyes to her. The house where she lived is also now gone.

The country around is still as beautiful and in spite of the changes and increased prosperity the character remains. That is a great heritage and, if your were born here, gives a feeling of belonging.

So we retrace our steps towards Dorchester but turn right at the road junction and proceed towards Grimstone. When we come to a little cottage on the corner of a narrow road that leads over the hill to Winterbourne Abass, I remember the number of times I walked that road on my way to my grandma's. We turn right under the railway arch taking the road to Sydling, but turn right again and make our way up to the station. But it has gone; it appears to be an oil depot and all semblance of a station has vanished. I felt rather sad and wished that some of those little old stations could have been preserved as mementoes of our past. They were so busy and hold so many poignant memories; the routine of shopping trips and the farewlls taken of those young men who went off to the war, many never to return. But that is the past and all too easily forgotten in the search for progress.

We drive on to Sydling, a lovely little village, which has hardly changed at all. Sometimes we would come here on Sunday mornings to listen to the Dorchester Salvation Army Band which came to play there on rare occasions.

It is very difficult to express the emotions that are stirred by returning to my native county after so many years and truly amazing how the memories revive as one visits haunts of the past. Many of the older houses remain and what tales they could tell if they could speak.

One fact I must record is the welcome I received from the people I met around Godmanstone and Bushes and I must record the names of those good people who planned my second return to Bushes Bottom - Mr Tim Mills of Watcome Farm; Mr Christopher Pope; Mrs Jean Morris of Huish Farm, Sydling, who now owns the farmstead at Bushes Barn; Mr Will Best of Manor Farm, Godmanstone; Mrs Morris's son John and her daugher, who all took part in what to me was a complete surprise.

After my first return to Bushes Bottom I wrote of life as it was there seventy years before. These good people had a copy of this little booklet (which is the central part of this book) and seemed most appreciative and I was invited to contact them on my return the following year. When I did so I got in touch with Mrs Morris and called on her at Sydling. I learned that on the following evening they had arranged for a tree to be planted by myself at Bushes. It was a lovely evening and all those already mentioned were there as well as a number of young people. John Morris and I dug a hole on the mound where we used to sit and listen to the gramophone. There I planted the beach tree they had supplied and then, to my astonishment, a brass plaque on a stand was produced and driven into the ground in front of the tree stating that I had planted the tree and had lived there from 1909-1914.

I cannot describe how I felt. I was very moved and realised that in spite of what had happened to the valley these people had a deep love of the countryside. The planting was toasted in champagne and wine supplied by Mr Pope and we chatted of times long gone. It is a memory that will always remain with me and my daughter and grandsons. A few days later Mr Pope took us over his estate and I could again see the valley I loved in the beautiful valley he took us to.

I now go back to Bushes Bottom every year. The kindness of Mrs Morris makes this possible and I am deeply grateful to her for her interest and help. We return to our home in the Midlands but as long as I am able I shall keep returning to my native homeland.

I am also fortunate to have a photograph of the farmstead before it was destroyed and an artist friend has made an enlarged sketch of it which we have had framed. I owe this to Mrs Gillard of Sherborne who read my little booklet and wrote telling me about the photo. She is the granddaughter of George Crabb the postmaster at Godmanstone.

Now after all these years I can return to Dorset and travel in comfort, visit old haunts and stand by the river listening to the tinkling of the water as it slowly moves in a never-ending journey; and it seems to be whispering of those memories of so long ago. Or I can go back to my valley and gaze at the ruins of the house in which I once lived with my parents, brother and sisters and here the brooding silence seems to symbolise what has gone for ever from the way of life of the past.

Last summer I went to the top of Crete Hill to see the sculpture which Will Best and others had erected. It is a splended idea and I wish that Mr Christopher Pope would rejuvenate Jackman's Cross. It should be preserved as it is part of our heritage. It marks the track which the old monks took when they travelled from Sherborne to Abbotsbury. Traces remain all along the tops of these hills and the clearest part of the trail is at Crete Hill.

That afternon I walked to the brow of the hill and looked down into the valley of Bushes Bottom at the remains of the farmstead and understood the meaning of a verse written by Henry Fancis Lighte when he was approaching the end of his life at Brixham. Here was I, eighty-five years old, gazing down at a scene full of childhood memories and hearing the words in my mind:

Swift to its close ebbs out life's little day
earth's joys grow dim, its glories pass away
change and decay in all around I see
Oh, Thou who changes not, abide with me.

I am not a religious person but these words seem so applicable to my experience that I never return without them flooding into my mind.

These are memories of long ago. Life in these districts will never be the same again. Everything changes, sometimes for the better, sometimes for the worse. I often wonder what my grandparents and parents would have thought of life today.

However one thing that never changes is the beauty of the steep hills and lonely valleys of my native county. Dorset remains a very beautiful county. I sincerely hope that future generations will share this feeling and work to preserve the beauties for all time.

Memories have been stirred and deep emotions experienced and the changes that have taken place merely confirm that nothing stands still and change is inevitable to the continuance of daily life. It is the path of progress to new ways of living, of ideas and methods, and I ask myself, 'did I expect to find things as I had left them seventy years ago'. The answer is, of course, no, it couldn't be. In accepting this fact I am reminded of the last lines of a poem my mother often quoted, they say it all:

Take this proverb to thine heart
Take and hold it fast
The mill will never grind
With water that has passed.

The ways of life must change with the passing years but the memories I have recorded here can remain and be shared by future generations.

WESSEX MEMORIES

BUSHES BARN

A more than half hour's walk from any road
the ruin stands, cradled in the downfold.
Ribbed pleats mitigate the strongest winds
seasonably chalk-white, green or gold.
Nearby a sapling beech commemorates
six years, 1909 - 1914
when R.C. Forcey lived here,
spelling in memoriam paradise.

Between my toes the long grass cool and stiff,
a decaying log, home of infinite
generations of grubs, provides a chair
near the one remaining gable. I sit
long afternoons away, accompanied
by liquid cooing, rhythm syncopated
with soft melancholy bleats
and lives passed here and there and somewhere else.

Enthralled the child chases the transient
beauty of the butterfies, rides the plough,
colossus among peers, tries his hand
at shearing, calls "Mam I'm hungry" bread baked
from the corn which ripples on the hill, gold
as the gorse whose faggots fired the stove,
tasting the first tart bramble wordless wishes
that the moment captured never passes.

I think of him as Robert that being my father's name
who could have lived such way if his mother
on being widowed had not sold the farm;
then would I too, or some other I,
child of my father by another wife
have passed a childhood bound by corn and ewes.
Tangle of roots, ifs and buts and wherefores
spinning kaleidoscopically.

The barns secretly replenished are mute,
silenced by ovine carcasses the well
his pains and pleasures his as mine are mine.
Long grass and the ash leaves rustling, hushing,
behind the green black buds already swell.
Sunwarmed I sleep and write and sleep again
half heard noises conjuring images,
wheat and sheep, sheep and wheat, wheaten sheep.

Ann Elton